Russia

Tradition, Culture, and Daily Life

MAJOR NATIONS IN A GLOBAL WORLD

Books in the Series

Russia

Tradition, Culture, and Daily Life

MAJOR NATIONS IN A GLOBAL WORLD

Michael Centore

Mason Crest

Mason Crest
450 Parkway Drive, Suite D
Broomall, PA 19008
www.masoncrest.com

Printed and bound in the United States of America.

First printing
9 8 7 6 5 4 3 2 1

Series ISBN: 978-1-4222-3339-9
ISBN: 978-1-4222-3349-8
ebook ISBN: 978-1-4222-8589-3

The Library of Congress has cataloged the hardcopy format(s) as follows:

Library of Congress Cataloging-in-Publication Data

Centore, Michael.
  Russia / by Michael Centore.
    pages cm
  Includes index.

  ISBN 978-1-4222-3349-8 (hardback) -- ISBN 978-1-4222-3339-9 (series) -- ISBN 978-1-
4222-8589-3 (ebook)
  1. Russia (Federation)--Juvenile literature. 2. Russia (Federation)--Social life and customs--
Juvenile literature. 3. Russia (Federation)--Civilization--Juvenile literature. I. Title.
  DK510.23.C43 2014
  947--dc23
                              2015005032

Developed and produced by MTM Publishing, Inc.
        Project Director   Valerie Tomaselli
        Copyeditor   Lee Motteler/Geomap Corp.
        Editorial Coordinator   Andrea St. Aubin

Indexing Services   Andrea Baron, Shearwater Indexing

Art direction and design by Sherry Williams, Oxygen Design Group

Contents

KEY ICONS TO LOOK FOR:

Words to Understand: These words with their easy-to-understand definitions will increase the reader's understanding of the text, while building vocabulary skills.

Sidebars: This boxed material within the main text allows readers to build knowledge, gain insights, explore possibilities, and broaden their perspectives by weaving together additional information to provide realistic and holistic perspectives.

Research Projects: Readers are pointed toward areas of further inquiry connected to each chapter. Suggestions are provided for projects that encourage deeper research and analysis.

Text-Dependent Questions: These questions send the reader back to the text for more careful attention to the evidence presented there.

Series Glossary of Key Terms: This back-of-the book glossary contains terminology used throughout this series. Words found here increase the reader's ability to read and comprehend higher-level books and articles in this field.

A Russian Orthodox church during winter in Vologda.

MAJOR NATIONS IN A GLOBAL WORLD: RUSSIA

INTRODUCTION

Sprawling from the Baltic Sea to the Bering Strait, the land of Russia occupies a grand place on the world's stage geographically, politically, and culturally. Its dramatic shifts in landscape encompass flat, grassy steppes and the stunning peaks of the Caucasus Mountains, dense hardwood forests, and the frozen wilds of Siberia. Throughout its long history Russia has assimilated ideas from various parts of the world, including Western Europe and the Byzantine Empire. This plus its diverse array of ethnic and religious groups all contribute to a unique national culture.

Like the epic scale of its countryside, Russia's sociopolitical history is one of extremes. It has seen monarchial dynasties, wars, and violent revolutions. Its experiment with Communism was born of high ideals of the equality of man, yet today it is the most economically imbalanced nation on earth. Despite this, many of the Russian people remain hopeful for their country's future. They know they have a rich if complex heritage from which to draw many lessons. Their ability to embrace different ideologies is what gives them their collective strength. To journey through the history of Russia is to witness the ambitions, struggles, and successes of an endlessly fascinating people.

Orthodox Christians participate in the consecration of water for a christening holiday in Moscow.

WORDS TO UNDERSTAND

advocate: to plead for the cause of something.

encompass: to envelop or include.

facilitate: to help bring about; to make easier.

precursor: something that indicates the approach of something else.

statecraft: the ideas about and methods of running a country.

thunderous: extremely great and intense.

CHAPTER 1

History, Religion, and Tradition

At 6.6 million square miles (17.1 million square km), Russia is by far the largest nation on earth. Its sheer size brings it into close proximity with a variety of lands and cultures, from China and Mongolia in the southeast to Finland in the northwest. Such breadth has assured it a prominent place in world affairs for centuries, with a dramatic history that **encompasses** periods of empire, war, and revolution.

The origins of modern Russia can be traced to the East Slavs, a migratory group that began to inhabit areas of present-day western Russia in the early centuries of the first millennium BCE. The East Slavs remain relatively obscure to historians, as they lacked a written language and thus a way to track their

The painting *The Invitation of the Varangians* by Viktor Vasnetsov depicts the arrival of Rurik and his brothers at the hands of the Ilmen Slavs.

history. By the seventh century they had become the most populous group in the region, and by the ninth century they had organized several tribal centers. These were **precursors** of the modern Russian city.

As the East Slavs were establishing their roots in the region, a group known as the Varangians (the East Slavic word for Vikings) sailed across the Baltic Sea to eastern Europe. Their leader, the chieftain Rurik, took control of the Slavic city of Novgorod in 862. Twenty years later his successor, Oleg, expanded Varangian power southward to the city of Kiev. This marked the beginnings of Kievan Rus', the first formal East Slavic state. With a shared interest in developing trade routes along the Dnieper River, the East Slavs and the Varangians soon unified. They controlled the flow of goods between Scandinavia and the Byzantine Empire. Kievan Rus' began a rise to prominence that would last more than two centuries.

Perhaps the most influential leader of Kievan Rus' was Vladimir I, a descendent of Oleg who forcefully seized power in 980. As grand prince of Kiev, Vladimir I led many military campaigns to expand the size of Kievan Rus'. What truly defined his legacy was his conversion from paganism to Christianity in 988. He wanted to unify his growing empire under a single religion and sent representatives to neighboring countries to investigate different faiths. He decided against Islam because it prohibited alcohol, a substance he felt would be difficult for his subjects to forsake. Judaism and Western Christianity were rejected as well. Vladimir's representatives were most impressed by the Orthodox Christians of the Byzantine Empire, based in Constantinople.

Vladimir led a military campaign into the Byzantine Empire, where he demanded to marry the sister of the Byzantine emperor Basil II. The emperor insisted that he be baptized into Orthodoxy. Vladimir promptly agreed, and his conversion was complete. He and his new bride returned to Kiev and began to purge the city of all pagan elements. In September 988, he had the population of Kiev baptized in the Dnieper River. Kievan Rus' was officially Orthodox, a decision that would shape the life of the Russian people for centuries to come.

This 1890 fresco painting by Viktor Vasnetsov depicts Vladimir's baptism.

VLADIMIR THE SAINT

For his contributions to the spread of Christianity, Vladimir I was canonized (made a saint) by the Russian Orthodox Church in the years following his death. He is the patron saint of Russian Catholics, and his feast day is celebrated on July 15.

In the eleventh century, Kievan Rus' reached its apex under the reign of Prince Yaroslav the Wise. This was a period of great achievement in architecture, church and social life, and legal studies. Despite this, the state began to splinter after Yaroslav's death. Smaller tribal clans began to assert more power. This left Kievan Rus' open to invasion by the Mongol Empire by the middle of the thirteenth century. The Mongols (as well as their allies, the Tatars) ruled over Kievan Rus' until 1480. During this time the city of Moscow surpassed Kiev as the center of political power. Ivan IV, then the grand duke of Moscow, made himself the first tsar in 1547. Known as "Ivan the Terrible," he consolidated the power of

Tourists gather in an elaborate hall in the Great Wooden Palace of Tsar Aleksey Mikhailovich (Mikhail I) Romanov in Kolomenskoe.

Eighteenth-century portrait of Tsar Aleksey Mikhailovich by Johann Vedikind.

the monarchy, restructured the military, and nearly doubled the size of Russia with his **thunderous** campaigns.

The death of Ivan IV in 1584 left the state in disarray. Several would-be rulers tried to claim the throne, but none with any legitimacy. An invasion by nearby Poland as well as a period of famine further complicated things. In 1613 the remaining nobility appointed Mikhail Romanov as the new tsar. The Romanov dynasty would rule Russia for the next 300 years.

PAST ALLIANCES

The Tatars were Turkic-speaking peoples located primarily in central Asia. Many joined the armies of Mongol leader Genghis Khan in the thirteenth century. The alliance between the Turks and the Mongols dominated the central Asian region until Russian power began to expand in the sixteenth century.

Under the first few generations of Romanovs, little changed in Russia. It was not until Peter the Great assumed full power in 1696 that Russia began to modernize. Peter was a very driven man, determined to make Russia a world power. During a two-year sojourn to Western Europe, he was able to study new methods of industry and **statecraft** firsthand, as well as experience European culture. He even disguised himself as a carpenter while traveling so that he could get closer to new systems of construction. He brought his findings back to Russia, swiftly instituting a series of changes that included outlawing traditional dress, updating the alphabet and calendar, and building technical schools. He even banned beards, long a favored feature of the nobility! His grandest undertaking was establishing a new Russian capital on the Gulf of Finland. St. Petersburg took nine years to complete and cost the country a great deal, both financially and in the number of lives lost during construction.

Portrait of Catherine the Great, by Russian painter Fyodor Rokotov (1763), oil on canvas.

Subsequent rulers of the Romanov dynasty, such as Catherine the Great, built upon Peter's advances. Russia became a fully formed empire, expanding into central Europe and southward along the coast of the Black Sea. In the nineteenth century it acquired territories in Asia and built the famed Trans-Siberian railway to **facilitate** transport across its many regions. At its peak, the Russian Empire was among the largest in world history, spanning three continents.

THE TWO PARTIES

Bolshevik comes from the Russian word *bol'shinstvo*, which means "one of the majority." *Menshevik*, alternatively, derives from *men'shinstvo*, or "one of the minority."

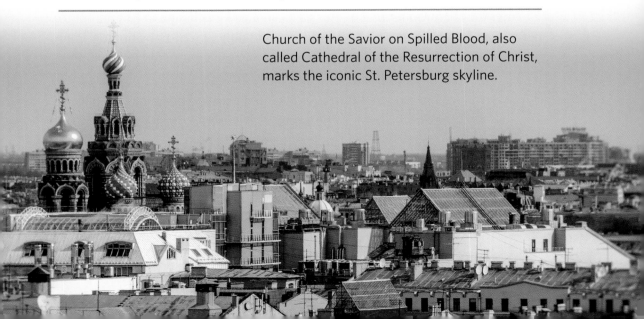

Church of the Savior on Spilled Blood, also called Cathedral of the Resurrection of Christ, marks the iconic St. Petersburg skyline.

An artistic rendering of Bloody Sunday, January 22, 1905, considered a critical event leading to the Russian Revolution of 1917. It depicts unarmed demonstrators marching to present a petition to Tsar Nicholas II being shot by the Imperial Guard at the Winter Palace.

At the dawn of the twentieth century, the social structure of the empire started to shift. A new class of workers who had emerged during Russia's period of industrialization began **advocating** for a greater say in the affairs of commerce and government. These workers banded together into councils known as "soviets," which in turn joined up with the Social-Democratic Workers' Party. The party split into two wings: the radical Bolsheviks and the more moderate Menshiviks. By 1917, after World War I had ravaged the Russian people, the Bolsheviks were poised to take power. In February they forced then-emperor Nicholas II to abdicate his throne. Under the direction of Vladimir Lenin, they seized control of the government in St. Petersburg that October. Subsequently renamed the Communist Party, this political entity would control Russian life for the bulk of the century, not formally dissolved until December 1991.

After the fall of Communism, Russia faced many challenges in its attempt to reintegrate into Western capitalist society. The difficulty of transitioning from state-owned to privately owned enterprises resulted in unemployment and other economic crises. Over time Russia has managed to rebuild itself into a world superpower. Today its economy is the ninth largest in the world, and it controls vast amounts of oil and gas reserves. The grand ambitions of its history continue to influence Russian life in the twenty-first century.

This 1956 stamp depicts Vladimir Lenin, one of the founding figures of the Russian Revolution.

TEXT-DEPENDENT QUESTIONS

1. What do you think contributed to Kievan Rus's rapid ascent to power?

2. How did Peter the Great seek to modernize Russia?

3. Why do you think workers rebelled against the Russian Empire at the beginning of the twentieth century?

RESEARCH PROJECTS

1. Select a leader from a period of Russian history (e.g., Kievan Rus', the Russian Empire, or the Communist Party) and research the person's life. Write a short biography that includes some of the changes he or she made to Russian life.

2. Research the events that led to the Russian Revolution. Write a brief report summarizing your findings. Be sure to include how the revolution reshaped the political landscape of Russia, and what its legacy has been.

A Russian church alongside a frozen river at dawn.

Women drink tea prepared in a traditional Russian samovar.

WORDS TO UNDERSTAND

candor: honest and sincere expression of feelings.

forage: to search for food or other provisions.

incarcerated: confined in prison usually for crimes committed.

repentance: the act of feeling regret for past actions coupled with the decision to change behavior.

rescind: to take away or reverse.

CHAPTER 2

Family and Friends

Russians are a very family-oriented people. They have a great deal of pride in their homeland and place a high value on familial roots. Extended families find time to congregate and celebrate birthdays, name days (marking the day of one's patron saint), and other events. Russians are known to cultivate strong, lasting friendships based in mutual **candor** and trust.

When a Russian family wishes to spend time together, a popular destination is a second home known as a dacha. In the late seventeenth century, Peter the Great began gifting pieces of land to loyal vassals. Thus the word "dacha" comes from the Russian verb *davat*, meaning "to give." The nobil-

Dachas, like this one, are popular with Russians wishing to escape the bustle of city life.

ity built dwellings on these pieces of land and used them as country retreats to escape the hectic pace of city life. By the nineteenth century, dachas had grown in popularity with members of the middle class. Dachas of all sizes—from huge mansions to humble buildings without running water—became places for Russians to rekindle their innate love for nature.

DACHA SUPERSTITIONS

Some superstitious beliefs have sprung up around dachas. One is that sleep in a wooden building is better for a person. Another is that the furniture of a dacha will be ruined by moonlight if left outside overnight.

With the rise of the Bolsheviks in 1917, dachas were seized by the government. The largest among them were redistributed amongst Communist Party leaders, while others were made available to workers, who could apply to use them as holiday retreats, though if the applicant displeased state leadership in any way, the privilege could be **rescinded**. There was little construction of new dachas until the 1950s. In the wake of World War II, Russians found the state could not provide enough food to meet their needs, and many took to farming on dachas to provide for their families. The state officially recognized their

efforts, and allowed people full access to the land to continue their agricultural endeavors. The construction of new dachas peaked in the 1980s, and they were again privatized in the 1990s. Today they remain an irreplaceable part of Russian social life.

The *banya*, a traditional steam bath, is a typical feature in the Russian dacha, or country house.

BANYA BENEFITS

Many dachas have *banyas*, or saunas, on their properties. The tradition of the *banya* is well established in Russia and in Slavic countries in general. They are said to have many medicinal properties, as hot steam helps clean the skin, remove impurities from the body, and improve immunity.

In urban areas, Russian families find alternate ways to entertain themselves. Since the fall of Communism, old-fashioned Russian folk holidays have grown in popularity. Russians have reincorporated them into the lives of their cities, often planning street festivals around them. Traditional Russian songs, dances, foods, and even styles of dress long suppressed by the Communist government have found new life at these celebrations. For instance, the festival of Ivan Kupalo (a Russian name for Saint John the Baptist) is celebrated in early July. People gather around bonfires and float wreaths adorned with lit candles along rivers.

Another activity Russians love to engage in is the art of mushroom hunting. The prime season for mushroom hunting is late August through the end of October. Families and friends will take to the forests around their dacha properties, wicker baskets

This 1880s oil painting, *Night on the Eve of Ivan Kupala* by Henryk Siemiradzki, depicts the Ivan Kupala Festival.

in hand, and try to locate some of the 200 varieties of edible mushrooms native to Russian soil. At the end of the day, they will bring their findings home to prepare one (or several) of the traditional mushroom-based dishes.

FAMOUS MUSHROOMS

Three of the most popular types of mushrooms found in Russia are the chanterelle, the porcini, and the oyster. A popular way to prepare all three is to sauté them in butter or oil.

Mushrooms have a long and storied history in Russian culture. With the rise of the Orthodox Church in the tenth century, they became the chosen replacement for meat during the Lenten fast. They have also helped people make it through times of food shortages. It is a rite of passage for Russian elders to show the younger members of their families the techniques of mushroom gathering, such as where particular mushrooms grow in the forest, which ones are poisonous and which are edible, and how to properly harvest them without disrupting the natural environment. Some Russians will even plan family trips to specific regions known for their mushrooms or plan overnight excursions in the woods to get an early start on the day's **foraging**.

Like the dacha itself, mushroom hunting represents for Russians a connection to the land. As the country continues to modernize, it is a tradition that ties people to their ancestral roots. Recipes for dishes such as mushroom-and-potato soup are passed from one generation to the next. Russians who have emigrated to other countries, including the United States, have taken the practice with them. It is a way for them to stay connected to their homeland while introducing this very useful skill to other cultures.

Chanterelles, popular with Russians who plan mushrooming outings in the countryside.

Easter Sunday, known as Pascha in the Orthodox Church, is the high point of the Orthodox year. It celebrates Christ's resurrection from the dead and, as such, is a very joyful time for families and friends. Preceding Pascha is the forty-day period known as Lent, during which all meat and dairy products are banned. As Lent draws to a close, a feeling of anticipation for Pascha begins. Traditionally, Russian believers use the week before the great feast to clean their homes and make any necessary repairs. Coupled with this is an "internal cleansing," as Russians prepare their minds and souls through prayer and **repentance**.

The start of Pascha is at midnight on Saturday. Families attend churches for a vigil service, featuring singing, processions, and candle-lighting rituals. On Sunday morning, the feast begins. People travel to each other's houses, distributing dyed eggs as a symbol of new life. Many believers still maintain the custom of visiting the poor or the **incarcerated** to share food and Paschal blessings. Families may also visit the graves

Russian Easter eggs painted in typically elaborate designs.

The Easter, or Pascha, celebration in the Russian Orthodox Church, such as the service shown here, takes place at midnight on Saturday, ushering in Christ's resurrection.

Families and friends gather for an afternoon Easter feast in Moscow.

of loved ones, leaving eggs as tribute and chanting prayers. The communal meal that afternoon features *kulich*, a sweet bread with raisins and almonds that is sometimes adorned with the image of a cross, and *pascha*, a creamed cheese spread often molded into the shape of a pyramid. Lamb or ham is also served. The jovial atmosphere is preserved in the weeks following Pascha as families and friends celebrate the renewals of spring.

The traditional *pascha* cream cheese spread surrounded by Easter eggs.

THE FUTURE IS BRIGHT

The week following Pascha is known as Bright Week. It is a time to prolong the Paschal celebration. Church readings are sung, and fasting restrictions are lifted.

TEXT-DEPENDENT QUESTIONS

1. How did the relationship between the Russian people and their dachas change with the rise of the Bolsheviks in 1917?

2. Why does mushroom hunting remain a popular pastime for families and friends in Russia?

3. How do Russian Paschal traditions connect to the season of spring?

RESEARCH PROJECTS

1. Research one of the Russian artists, writers, poets, or painters known to have inhabited a dacha at some point. (Boris Pasternak, Maxim Gorky, and Alexander Pushkin are just a few examples.)

   How did the experience shape his or her work?

2. Research a Russian Orthodox church located in America, perhaps even in your city or state. Has it maintained many of the same Paschal traditions outlined above? If not, how have these traditions changed?

A choir singing in Moscow during Shrovetide, a traditional Russian Orthodox holiday during Maslenitsa.

Foods for a traditional Russian feast.

WORDS TO UNDERSTAND

artisanal: something produced by skilled artists or craftspeople.

attune: to adapt to a specific moment or time.

bemoan: to express grief or displeasure.

infuse: to cause to be permeated, or blended, with something.

perennial: present throughout all seasons of the year; continuing uninterruptedly.

CHAPTER 3

Food and Drink

Hearty cuisine is a vital part of Russian life. Having to endure long, cold winters means that Russians seek out food to provide warmth and stores of energy. Dishes such as pirozhki (pastries stuffed with rich fillings like potatoes, cheese, or meat) and borsht (a beet soup served either hot or cold, often with a dollop of sour cream) are **perennial** staples of the Russian diet. Vodka, caviar, and kasha (a cereal usually made of buckwheat grains) are other favorites.

Tea, by far, is the beverage of choice in Russia. It is estimated that 82 percent of Russians consume the beverage daily. Discovered in China in the third century BCE, tea did not arrive in Russia until the seventeenth century, when the Chinese ambassador to Moscow gifted tea chests to Tsar Alexis I. Soon tea was

These pirozhki pastries are stuffed with cabbage and eggs and served alongside a cup of tea.

Vodka and caviar with bread are Russian favorites as well.

a desired commodity among the Russians. An arduous trade route between China and Russia drove the price of the product up, and for many years tea could only be acquired by the very rich. By the end of the eighteenth century, it became more accessible to all of Russian society. It was instantly popular, and by the nineteenth century Russia began importing varieties from Odessa and London to meet demand.

TEA AND . . .

It is considered impolite to serve tea in Russia without some type of accompaniment. Russians will usually offer their guests baked goods such as pastries, though savory items like sausage can be served instead.

Black tea remains the preferred type in Russia today. A unique blend known as Russian Caravan got its name from being transported on camel caravans from China to Russia; the infusing of the traders' campfires into the tea over the long journey gave it a particularly smoky flavor. Customarily, Russians prefer these strong brews with a bit of sugar, honey, or even jam to add sweetness.

No Russian home is complete without a samovar, a metal container used to boil water for tea. The traditional samovar is shaped like an urn and has a hollow cylinder in the center. The urn is filled with water and the cylinder is filled with fuel such as wood chips or dried pinecones, which are lit to heat the water. When one desires a cup of tea, he or she pours a small amount of highly concentrated brew from a teapot, then dilutes it with the heated water from a spout at the base of the samovar. While most samovars today are powered by electricity, the practice of gathering around them to share tea and conversation remains deeply engrained in Russian life.

A RUSSIAN FIXTURE

Samovars are so common in Russia, in fact, that they are even located in train stations for passengers who wish for a quick cup of tea on their travels.

Even in Russia—not a place necessarily known for warm weather—there are times when one simply wishes to quench his or her thirst, and hot tea will not do. In these instances, the go-to beverage is kvass: a fizzy drink made of fermented bread that is sometimes referred to as the "Russian cola." Kvass (meaning "leaven") dates back to the tenth century, though the technique of

A samovar adorned with bread rolls, an essential when drinking tea.

Going to a kvass street vendor, like this one in Belgorod, in western Russia, is an easy way to enjoy the traditional beverage.

making fermented beverages is at least 5,000 years old. To make kvass in the traditional way, the producer begins with brown bread moistened with water. Yeast, raisins, and herbs such as mint are added; other recipes call for honey, ginger, lemon, or other flavoring agents. After a fermentation process that lasts a few days, the liquid carbonates naturally. It is then strained and stored, and after two or three days' additional fermentation it is ready to drink. In the summer, kvass vendors populate the street corners of Russian cities, selling the beverage out of large, colorful tanks.

After the fall of Communism, when Western-style sodas were introduced to Russia, kvass had a momentary dip in popularity. After the novelty wore off, kvass experienced a resurgence. Large soft drink companies began making and marketing it to meet demand. Since kvass is a "live beverage," meaning it contains bacteria that trigger the fermentation process, it is difficult to produce on a large scale without using

Made from bread, kvass is a filling and satisfying drink.

sugar and artificial additives. The result is an overly sweet, inauthentic-tasting version. Many Russians **bemoan** the commercialization of the product. In response, small-scale suppliers have begun to make kvass using time-honored **artisanal** methods.

MONK KVASS
Some of the finest kvass is made in Russian Orthodox monasteries. The monks of Savvino-Storozhevsky Monastery in Zvenigorod (approximately 35 miles, or 56 km, west of Moscow) have been brewing kvass for 600 years. Only in 2001 did they begin selling it to the public.

Of course, no one can live on beverages alone, though a key component of the Russian diet comes in liquid form: soup. Russians have a great appetite for soups of all kinds. It is often the first course served at lunch, the main meal of the day. Over the centuries, Russians have developed many types, each **attuned** to a particular time or season. There are cold soups, light soups of mostly vegetables, and heftier noodle soups with meat or mushrooms. Some

The monks of the Savvino-Storozhevsky Monastery pictured here are masters at making kvass.

A national dish of Russia, as well as the Ukraine, borscht can be served either hot or cold.

specialty soups include *rassolnik*, with kidneys and pickles, and *shchi*, a cabbage soup that is one of the country's most famous dishes. While every region has its own variation, the classic *shchi* contains cabbage, meat, root vegetables, a few spices, and sour cream.

The Russian soup known best outside of Russia, however, is borscht. This soup is said to have originated with the Cossacks (an East Slavic group that lived in present-day Ukraine and southern Russia), who created it as a way to feed their large military in the seventeenth century. The key ingredient in borscht is beets, which give it its characteristic reddish-purple color. Like *shchi*, recipes for borscht vary from region to region—and even from family to family, as one generation passes down its favored technique to the next. Borscht is very versatile in that it can be served both hot and cold. The hot version usually contains meat along with vegetables such as potatoes, onions, and carrots. Sometimes bacon is added to give further flavor. Cold borscht is a bit lighter and more refreshing. In place of meat, it includes additional fresh vegetables. Sour cream is often stirred into the soup, as well as hard-boiled eggs to provide more protein.

EAT YOUR BEETS!

Borscht is an incredibly nutritious dish, as beets contain high amounts of iron and other minerals. It is also known as a natural remedy for staving off the flu. Served with dense rye bread, a bowl can serve as a meal in itself.

TEXT-DEPENDENT QUESTIONS

1. Why is tea such a popular beverage in Russia, and what is the significance of drinking it communally out of a samovar?
2. Why have corporations begun to mass produce kvass? How has it changed the product?
3. Why might the soups that Russians eat vary season to season?

 # RESEARCH PROJECTS

1. Research the role of tea and tea-drinking ceremonies in another part of the world, such as England or India. Write a report explaining how this other culture's tea traditions differ from those of Russia.
2. Research recipes for borscht, either hot or cold. Attempt to follow one of these recipes. When you are done, write a report explaining your process, your impressions of the taste, and why you think it remains a staple in Russian cuisine.

Russian *pelmeni* (meat dumplings) with sour cream and dill.

A busy street market, typical in many towns and cities in Russia.

WORDS TO UNDERSTAND

iconic: relating to something that has become an emblem or symbo

metaphor: a figure of speech in which a word, phrase, or image is used to suggest something else.

serfdom: the practice of forcing a person, called a serf, to work for a landowner.

theorist: a person who proposes new ideas and ways of thinking.

unsustainable: prematurely depleting or damaging a natural resource.

CHAPTER 4

School, Work, and Industry

While the era of Communism set Russia behind a bit in the global economy, there is no doubt that it was and remains a nation of industrious residents. From oil and gas production to mining to large-scale agriculture, Russia has taken its place as an economic power. Though such practices as **serfdom**, which was not abolished until 1861, and forced labor camps during the Soviet era may complicate Russia's historical relationship with work, many of its political **theorists** believed in the dignity of the laborer and his or her contribution to society as a whole.

With its long tradition of philosophical, theological, and sociological thought, Russian culture has great respect for learning. One of its most storied

Students from the University of Humanities, in red, play volleyball against students from the University of Physical Education in Moscow, where over 6,000 students attend.

educational centers, however, is focused on a different sort of skill: dance. The Vaganova Ballet Academy is one of the oldest ballet schools in the world. It was founded as the Imperial Theatrical School in 1738 by the Empress Anna, and was initially based out of the Winter Palace in St. Petersburg. At first it had only twenty-four students, but within a few generations it grew significantly. Its principle role was to train dancers for the Imperial Russian Ballet (now called the Mariinsky Ballet), a world-renowned company officially formed in 1740. In 1836, the school moved to a more permanent location in St. Petersburg, and it has been there ever since.

PHYS ED RUSSIAN STYLE

Russian education does not end with the intellectual development of a child. Teachers are trained to consider the physical, emotional, and moral components of children's upbringing as well. Physical education was especially stressed during the Soviet era, and students were forced to pass physical tests to graduate. The current government is seeking to reinstate such tests to ensure students are sound in both body and mind.

Agippina Vaganova, for whom the famous ballet school was named, is pictured here dancing in *La Esmeralda* in St. Petersburg, circa 1910.

Today there are over 300 students at the academy. As it is fully supported by the Russian government, they pay no tuition. This makes for a very competitive admission process: anywhere from 4,000 to 7,000 children audition annually for a scant seventy spots. Students study not only ballet but do intensive work in other academic disciplines such as history, science, and languages. Evaluations can be brutal: if instructors do not feel a student is making progress, he or she will be asked to leave. Only a select few students even graduate, much less obtain placements with professional companies such as the Bolshoi Ballet in Moscow, one of the most famous in the world. Others may find positions with American companies, evidence of how globalization has linked formerly distant people and places.

While Vaganova is particularly renowned, the general education system in Russia is also well regarded. This is reflected in the country's 98 percent literary rate, among the highest in the world. School is mandatory for students between six and fifteen years of age. This is divided into primary school (through age ten) and secondary school components. At age fifteen, students can opt to enter either a vocational school or complete their secondary education at a nonuniversity institution. During the Soviet era, a great emphasis was placed on science and technology in both vocational and secondary school programs. Today, even after the breakup of the USSR, Russians are still highly trained in these fields; engineering and medicine are two well-regarded preprofessional programs.

Moscow's majestic Bolshoi Theater, with its classic fountain, is a shrine to the tradition of Russian excellence in ballet.

Russia's aerospace program has been, since its inception, one of the best in the world. It has been responsible for such achievements as sending the first human into space, the first satellite, and the first spacewalk.

This 1984 stamp shows the first Russian in space, Yuri Gagarin.

The Russian people's appreciation for their history and their innate respect for the value of labor come together in a rich tradition of arts and crafts. Woodcarving, toy making, and various types of decorative painting are all examples of Russian folk art. Yet it is the *matryoshka* doll that is perhaps the most **iconic**. Commonly known as "Russian nesting dolls," these are sets of wooden figures carved in decreasing size. The figures are split in two parts, and the top part can be removed to house another doll; thus the smaller dolls "nest" inside the larger ones.

The first set of Russian nesting dolls was produced in 1890. It featured eight figures and was inspired by a Japanese toy of similar design. The name "matryoshka" means "little matron," a reference to the fact that the outermost doll in most traditional sets is an elderly female. In fact, many Russians refer to these

An example of Russian nesting dolls, with their tiny but elaborately painted designs and images.

Women producing *matryoshkas*, or nesting dolls, in a studio in Nizhny Novgorod.

dolls as babushkas, which means "dear grandmother"—the image of a maternal doll "containing" several children serves as a beautiful visual **metaphor** for the continuity of life. The innermost doll in the set is often a baby made of a solid piece of wood.

DOLLS INSIDE DOLLS

While the traditional "matron" motif of the Russian nesting doll remains the most popular, modern artisans have crafted sets based on political figures, figures from fairy tales or religious parables, and popular actors and actresses. There is even a *matroyshka* set to commemorate the Beatles!

Most *matroyshka* dolls are carved from lime, birch, alder, or aspen wood. Logs are turned on a machine called a lathe, and using tools such as chisels and knives, the artisan gives each doll its shape. He or she must be very conscious of measurements, as the dolls have to fit tightly within each other. After the dolls are carved, they are given a thorough cleaning, coated with a special primer, and allowed to dry before being painted. This final step is a true display of artistry, as the painter must work on a very small, curved surface to create colored patterns of striking beauty.

Matroyshka dolls are not the only Russian product made of wood, of course, and the nation's forestry industry works incredibly hard to meet demand. Forests cover a full 45 percent of the Russian landscape and make up more than 20 percent of the world's forested area. It is no surprise that the timber industry generates approximately US$20 billion per year. While this is a small fraction of the country's annual gross domestic product—the total amount of money generated by all the various industries—logging still provides jobs to many Russians in rural, undeveloped areas.

A BOOMING TRADE IN TIMBER

China is the largest purchaser of Russian timber, which is used to build homes and other structures for its rapidly growing cities. Other high-volume buyers include Egypt and Uzbekistan. Russia remains the number one country in the world for industrial log exports.

Over the past decade, however, the industry has suffered due to years of **unsustainable** forestry practices such as clear-cutting. Environmental calamities including wildfires, droughts, and insect infestations have also had an impact. Loggers are torn between implementing modern, environmentally sound techniques that will provide long-term benefits and trying to meet the global demands of the timber trade, especially from China and Japan. Conservation associations from all over the world are currently working with Russians to find that perfect balance.

Graded, numbered, and debarked logs are ready for shipment.

TEXT-DEPENDENT QUESTIONS

1. Why is the Vaganova Ballet Academy such a well-known and storied institution?
2. Why do you think *matroyshka* dolls have such universal appeal?
3. What changes does the Russian forestry industry have to undergo in order to stay current in the global marketplace?

RESEARCH PROJECTS

1. Research an alumnus of the Vaganova Ballet Academy (Natalia Makarova, Anna Pavlova, and Vaslav Nijinsky are some examples). Write a short biography, being sure to include his or her signature dance performances.
2. Research another folk art tradition in Russia, such as wood carving or *khokhloma* painting. Write a summary of its history and significance in Russian culture, including any noteworthy practitioners.

Russian cargo train moving goods across the country.

The Russian Museum, established in 1895 in St. Petersburg.

WORDS TO UNDERSTAND

devotional: of or relating to the practice of prayer or worship.

genre: a category of artistic, musical, or literary composition.

iconographer: a person who paints icons.

idiom: the language particular to a community or class; usually refers to regular, "everyday" speech.

impromptu: done without being planned; spontaneous.

CHAPTER 5

Arts and Entertainment

From poetry to painting to newer forms such as film, Russian artists have made some truly lasting contributions to world culture. The notion of the "Russian soul" has come to represent art and literature that deals with universal themes such as love, death, and the relationship between the individual and society. In its unique geographical position as a "bridge" between East and West, Russia has forged its own identity, producing many singular figures of great insight. Even as their art and literature bears a distinct cultural imprint, Russians enjoy many other forms of entertainment, using their leisure time for recreational activities both intellectual and physical.

Russia (pictured) plays against Sweden at the 2012 World Bandy Championship in Almaty, Kazakhstan.

Russians turn to the ice for some of their leisure activity. Hockey is played by many and enjoyed by fans across the country. A related sport is bandy. This game has similarities to both soccer and hockey. It is played on large rinks the size of soccer fields, and each team has ten "field" players and one goalkeeper. Using curved sticks, the players attempt to shoot a small ball into the opposing team's goal. A major difference from hockey is that the goalkeeper does not use a stick; instead, he attempts to catch shots in his gloves or deflect them with his legs. The length of a bandy match is two halves of forty-five minutes each. More than a million Russians play bandy, as it suits the country's cold climate. There are amateur leagues for players of all ages. Thousands of fans turn out for professional bandy matches, making spectatorship of the sport another major form of Russian entertainment. International matches are also a big draw; the rivalry between Russia and Sweden is bandy's most intense.

In the arts, one of Russia's most revered figures is Andrei Rublev. Many Russians and non-Russians alike consider him to be the finest painter of icons of all time. An icon is a **devotional** object used by Orthodox Christians as an aid to prayer. It is an image of a saint or a scene from the life of Christ, often painted on wood, that attempts to convey the reality of the painter's religious experience. Orthodox Christians believe that icons are not works of art so much as "windows" into the deeper mysteries of their faith. **Iconographers** do not sign their creations, as they do not wish to draw attention to themselves, but rather they place all emphasis on the spiritual scene depicted. They must be vetted by Church officials to be considered true iconographers and must begin every project with a period of fasting and prayer.

The little we know of Andrei Rublev's biography shows he was well disposed for such a rigorous life. Born in the 1360s, he most likely became a monk at the Andronikov Monastery in Moscow. He soon began working alongside an iconographer named Theophanes the Greek. Together they painted frescoes (large paintings on plaster surfaces) and icons in various Russian churches and monasteries. Perhaps Rublev's most famous icon is a depiction of an Old Testament scene in which three angels came to visit the patriarch Abraham, known as the *Trinity* icon. It was painted for the cathedral of Saint Sergius Trinity Monastery in Sergiev Posad. Rublev died around 1430. Over the centuries his work has only grown in esteem. He was made a saint by the Russian Orthodox Church in 1988—the first painter ever to receive such an honor.

Pictured here is Andrei Rublev's famous *Trinity* icon.

Another artistic discipline where Russians have excelled is that of literature. Its "golden age" began with the poet Alexander Pushkin, whose long poem *Eugene Onegin* had great influence on subsequent Russian writers. Pushkin modernized the Russian language, unafraid to employ the **idioms** of his time. This led to a naturalistic, yet still highly poetic speech that was soon adopted by writers of many different **genres**.

THE HOME OF TOLSTOY

Leo Tolstoy's home, Yasnaya Polyana, is today a museum honoring his life and work. Located in the region of Tula south of Moscow, it has preserved, intact, his library of over 20,000 books.

It was the rise of two singular novelists, Leo Tolstoy and Fyodor Dostoyevsky, that brought Russian literature onto the world stage. Tolstoy's *War and Peace* (published in 1869), an epic account of the Napoleon's invasions of Russia in 1812 and their impact on various strata of Russian society, remains a touchstone of world literature. In the context of its broad, sweeping narrative, it confronted moral questions of war, patriotism, and personal responsibility with great intensity. *Anna Karenina*'s tale is of a woman torn between two men, followed in 1877 and remains widely regarded for its intimate portrayal of human love.

Like Tolstoy, Dostoyevsky's work looks deep into the human condition in all

Leo Tolstoy's home dusted with snow in Tula, Russia.

A Tolstoy family portrait shown here on a postcard.

of its stations. What sets him apart, however, is his rigorous focus on the psychological dimensions of his characters. In books like *Crime and Punishment* (1866), about a man with very tangled motives who murders an older woman, Dostoyevsky attempts to "get inside" people's minds and try to understand what makes them act the way they do. *The Brothers Karamazov* (1880) is his masterpiece, documenting the murder of an elderly Russian patriarch by one of his four sons—and the reader is left in suspense until the end to find out which one. With its searching questions about the nature of God's relationship to man, the book remains not just a

Oil portrait of Fyodor Dostoyevsky by Vasily Perov (1872).

towering literary achievement but a theological and philosophical one as well. It has been translated into several languages and read widely across the world.

AN EXILE OF INFLUENCE

In 1849 Dostoyevsky was exiled to the remote area of Siberia for his participation in a revolutionary group known as the Petrashevsky Circle. His eight years there, spent in a forced labor camp, were to be a lasting influence on his life and fiction.

By these artistic endeavors, one would think that Russians are a perpetually intense people, never making any time for fun. This would be a wrong assumption, however, when one considers the festive holiday of Maslenitsa. Originally a pagan celebration to welcome the arrival of spring, Maslenitsa has been, since the Christian era in Russia, a time of merrymaking before the harsh fasts of Lent. The name "Maslenitsa" comes from the Russian word for butter or oil,

Artists in costume celebrating the Maslenitsa festival in Izmaylovskiy Kremlin.

maslo. This refers to the tradition of preparing thin, sweet pancakes called blini for the festivities, as they contain all the ingredients banned during Lent: eggs, butter, and milk.

Maslenitsa lasts for a full week. Russians celebrate with a variety of winter activities: sledding, riding in sleighs through the countryside, and even putting on puppet shows and **impromptu** theatrical performances. On Wednesday, mothers-in-law invite their sons-in-law (and their families) to their homes for blini. The invitation is reciprocated on Friday, when sons-in-law do the cooking! The festival culminates on what is known as "Forgiveness Sunday," when people ask one another to pardon any transgressions of the past year. This is the final step in preparing for the long Lenten pilgrimage to come.

"CLEAN MONDAY"

The day after Maslenitsa is known as "Clean Monday," as everyone has confessed his or her sins. Traditionally it is marked by a ritual bath and by cleaning the dishes that have accumulated throughout the week.

People of all ages love the thin pancakes served during the springtime festival of Maslenitsa.

TEXT-DEPENDENT QUESTIONS

1. How do icons differ from traditional paintings?

2. What are some of the major themes of Russian literature, and why are they important today?

3. What are some Maslenitsa traditions?

RESEARCH PROJECTS

1. Research a Russian writer of your choosing. Write a brief biography, including his or her influences, interests, and themes. If you are inspired, read one of his or her works and record your impressions in the biography.

2. Research a Russian holiday, either civic or religious, and write a brief report describing how citizens celebrate it.

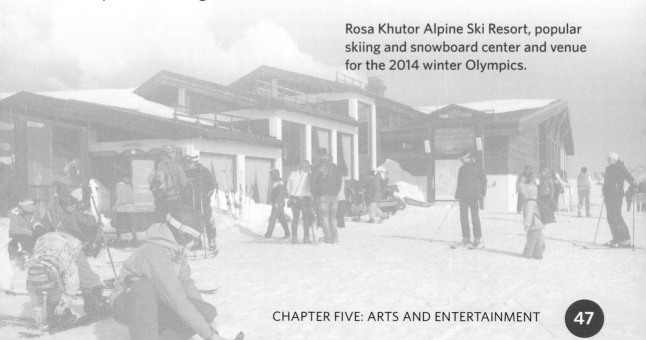

Rosa Khutor Alpine Ski Resort, popular skiing and snowboard center and venue for the 2014 winter Olympics.

Church of Saint John Chrysostom in Saunino village, in western Russia.

WORDS TO UNDERSTAND

constituent: serving to form, compose, or make up a unit or whole.

exacerbate: to make more violent, bitter, or severe.

grandeur: the quality or state of being grand; magnificence.

impasse: a road or way that cannot be crossed or surmounted.

precursor: something that precedes and indicates the approach of something else.

CHAPTER 6

Cities, Towns, and the Countryside

Russians place great importance on where they were born, be it a city, town, or village. Each has its own unique characteristics that impact a person's social station, customs, and beliefs. The history of rural areas, or provinces, in Russia is very different from that of major cities such as St. Petersburg or Moscow. Where the cities have largely adapted to modern trends, much of the countryside remains slow to progress. This divide has shaped the country's political and economic structure, among other things.

Perhaps the most well known of all Russian cityscapes, Moscow's Red Square brings together many strands of the country's history. And like many important urban spaces, it acts as a transportation hub as well, as the city's

Moscow's Red Square—a famous tourist haven and gathering place—with its iconic view of St. Basil's Cathedral, on the left, and the Kremlin.

The elaborate, colorful domes of St. Basil's Cathedral.

major roads converge on the site. On the west side of the square is the Kremlin—in Russian meaning "fortress within a city"—bordered by the Moscva River. The Kremlin's red brick fortifications have housed Russian leaders on and off since the 1500s. On the south end of the square is St. Basil's Cathedral, an exuberant representation of the Eastern Orthodox Church's enduring influence in Russia. On the east side is Kitai-gorod, the city's historic market district. Recognized by UNESCO as a World Heritage Site in 1990, the Red Square, along with the Kremlin, is truly a symbol of Russian history and culture, and as the site of national celebrations, military ceremonies, and political protests, it is one of the world's most vibrant public spaces.

Long a symbol of Russia's imperial legacy, the Winter Palace in St. Petersburg stands next to Moscow's Red Square as one of Russia's most famous urban landmarks. Located at Palace Square on the south bank of the Neva River, the original building on the site was a much humbler dwelling: a wooden home for Peter the Great, completed in 1708. A second, larger home was built three years later. Peter supervised refurbishments to this structure until his death in 1725. He was very influenced by European architecture and wanted to import some of its Baroque **grandeur** to Russia. Peter's descendents continued to expand the palace throughout the mid-eighteenth century, to the point that it was almost unrecognizable and became known as the "third" Winter

Palace. Finally, in 1753, the Empress Elizabeth Petrovna decreed that a fourth Winter Palace would be built on a truly grand scale. A temporary residence was constructed as architect Bartolomeo Francesco Rastrelli supervised the project.

WINTER PALACE GRANDEUR

It is believed that the Winter Palace contains 1,786 doors, 1,945 windows, and over a thousand rooms. Even with such an expansive floor plan, much of the building is open to the public.

Completed in 1762, this final version of the Winter Palace is three stories tall and takes up an entire city block. It is known for its ornate decorative elements, including statuary, both inside and out. Empress Elizabeth died before it was completed, though her successor, Catherine the Great, promptly added another wing known as the "Hermitage." This functioned as both a private living quarters and as a home for her expanding art collection. The Winter Palace was the seat of the Russian monarchy until 1917, when socialist revolutionaries seized power and made it the temporary home of their governing body. After a period of decline **exacerbated** by the hardships of World War II, the Winter Palace was restored in the 1950s. Today the Hermitage is one of the foremost art museums in the world, housing works from ancient Egypt through the modern period.

The Winter Palace in St. Petersburg as seen from the Neva River.

Though certain towns and villages in Russia are still quite remote, the country is much more connected in modern times due to the advent of the railway system. The first railway built in Russia was begun in 1842 under the direction of Tsar Nicholas I. It took nine years to complete, but by 1851 there was a direct line between the two major cities of St. Petersburg and Moscow. Rail construction boomed over the next forty years, as engineers expanded the system to include parts of Russia on the European and Central Asian borders. All of this was a **precursor**, however, to what would be the greatest challenge yet: the construction of the Trans-Siberian Railway, which began in 1891 and was not fully completed until 1916.

ACROSS RUSSIA ON ROLLING STOCK

The Trans-Siberian Railway crosses eight time zones and is longer than the Great Wall of China. Every year, 20,000 containers are shipped to Europe on its line. A full journey from Moscow to Vladivostok takes a week to complete.

At 5,722 miles (9,207 km), the Trans-Siberian Railway is the longest in the world. It stretches from Moscow in the west to the city of Vladivostok—not far from the Chinese border—in the east. The genesis of the project came from Tsar Alexander III, who recognized that maintaining a connection to (and influence over) Siberian territory was essential for Russia to maintain its status in the world. Construction was incredibly difficult, as the route traversed frozen landscapes and mountainous terrain. In addition, bridges and tunnels had to be built to get over water or through **impasses**. Workers—mostly prisoners or soldiers—tirelessly laid down over 350 miles (563 km) of track per day. An initial route that passed through Manchuria, China, was completed by 1905. A second route that runs entirely through Russia was completed soon thereafter, in 1916. The railway connected the hinterlands of Siberia with the rest of Russia, thus opening the region up to economic development and settlement.

The Circum-Baikal Railway, part of the Trans-Siberian rail system, along Lake Baikal.

Today the Trans-Siberian Railway is used to send freight between Europe and the Far East, at a speed considerably less than by boat. It is also a popular way for travelers to see remote towns and villages of Russia that would otherwise be inaccessible: places such as Ulan-Ude (the center of Buddhism in the country) and Irkutsk (close to the beautiful Lake Baikal, the deepest freshwater lake in the world) are just two potential stops along the epic journey.

The vast size of Russia makes it difficult to have a centralized, uniform system for civic administration. As such, the nation is divided into smaller **constituent** parts called "federal subjects." There are currently eighty-five federal subjects of Russia, though two of these—the Republic of Crimea and the federal city of Sevastopol—are not recognized by many in the international community, as they are technically located in the nation of Ukraine and under its jurisdiction.

"ORGANIZING" A VAST COUNTRY

The largest federal subject of Russia by population is the federal city of Moscow, with 11.5 million residents. The smallest is the autonomous *okrug* of Nenets, with 42,000.

There are six types of Russian federal subjects. Twenty-one of these (excluding Crimea) are republics, which means that they are home to people of an ethnicity other than Russian. They can maintain their own language and create their own

Ivolginsky datsan, the Buddhist temple in Buryatia, a center of Tibetan Buddhism in Russia east of Lake Baikal.

A panoramic view of Moscow.

constitution. There are also forty-six provinces known as oblasts, which are run by elected legislatures supervised by governors; nine territories (or *krais*), similar to oblasts in their governing structure; four autonomous districts (or *okrugs*), which are home to specific ethnic populations; two federal cities (excluding Sevastopol); and the Jewish Autonomous Oblast. While the arrangement is rather complicated, having locally based leadership in each of the subjects helps facilitate relations with Moscow, the center of Russian governance.

OLYMPIC PROPORTIONS

In preparation for the 2014 Winter Olympics held in Sochi, on the coast of the Black Sea, Russian rail workers were hired for a series of new projects. They built seventeen new tunnels and laid nearly 100 miles (160 km) of new track in the vicinity of the city. This helped increase train frequency to deal with the influx of visitors.

The main square of Vologda in northwest Russia seen from the Vologda River.

TEXT-DEPENDENT QUESTIONS

1. What sorts of changes has the Winter Palace undergone over the centuries? How have they contributed to public access of the building?
2. How has the Trans-Siberian railway unified the nation of Russia, and what has it done in particular for the region of Siberia?
3. Why is it useful for the Russian government to divide the nation into federal subjects?

RESEARCH PROJECTS

1. Research the route of the Trans-Siberian Railway and create an itinerary for a possible journey. List where you would want to stop and why, and what scenery, cities, or people you might hope to encounter.
2. Research one of the federal subjects of Russia—either a republic, oblast, *krai*, *okrug*, federal city, or autonomous oblast—and write a brief report telling of its history, native population, form of governance, and current relationship with the rest of Russia.

Typical rural village in Russia.

FURTHER RESEARCH

Online

View statistics, maps, and a brief history of Russia on the Central Intelligence Agency's World Factbook (https://www.cia.gov/library/publications/the-world-factbook/geos/rs.html).

Visit RusCuisine (http://ruscuisine.com) to learn more about authentic Russian foods and to explore recipes.

The official government website of the Russian Federation (http://government.ru/en/about/) provides up-to-date information about government decisions, legislation, and interactions with the world.

Go to the Russian National Group's Russia Travel website (http://www.russia-travel.com) to learn more about Russian tourism.

The US Department of State hosts a site about Russia (http://www.state.gov/p/eur/ci/rs/), featuring fact sheets and press releases about US–Russian relations.

Books

Barker, Adele Marie, and Bruce Grant, eds. *The Russia Reader: History, Culture, Politics.* Durham, NC: Duke University Press, 2010.

Feifer, Gregory. *Russians: The People behind the Power.* New York: Twelve Books, 2014.

Frazier, Ian. *Travels in Siberia.* New York: Picador, 2011.

Tolstoy, Leo. *Tolstoy's Short Fiction.* New York: W. W. Norton & Company, 2008.

Von Bremzen, Anya. *Mastering the Art of Soviet Cooking: A Memoir of Food and Longing.* New York: Broadway Books, 2014.

NOTE TO EDUCATORS: This book contains both imperial and metric measurements as well as references to global practices and trends in an effort to encourage the student to gain a worldly perspective. We, as publishers, feel it's our role to give young adults the tools they need to thrive in a global society.

SERIES GLOSSARY

ancestral: relating to ancestors, or relatives who have lived in the past.

archaeologist: a scientist that investigates past societies by digging in the earth to examine their remains.

artisanal: describing something produced on a small scale, usually handmade by skilled craftspeople.

colony: a settlement in another country or place that is controlled by a "home" country.

commonwealth: an association of sovereign nations unified by common cultural, political, and economic interests and traits.

communism: a social and economic philosophy characterized by a classless society and the absence of private property.

continent: any of the seven large land masses that constitute most of the dry land on the surface of the earth.

cosmopolitan: worldly; showing the influence of many cultures.

culinary: relating to the kitchen, cookery, and style of eating.

cultivated: planted and harvested for food, as opposed to the growth of plants in the wild.

currency: a system of money.

demographics: the study of population trends.

denomination: a religious grouping within a faith that has its own organization.

dynasty: a ruling family that extends across generations, usually in an autocratic form of government, such as a monarchy.

ecosystems: environments where interdependent organisms live.

endemic: native, or not introduced, to a particular region, and not naturally found in other areas.

exile: absence from one's country or home, usually enforced by a government for political or religious reasons.

feudal: a system of economic, political, or social organization in which poor landholders are subservient to wealthy landlords; used mostly in relation to the Middle Ages.

globalization: the processes relating to increasing international exchange that have resulted in faster, easier connections across the world.

gross national product: the measure of all the products and services a country produces in a year.

heritage: tradition and history.

homogenization: the process of blending elements together, sometimes resulting in a less interesting mixture.

iconic: relating to something that has become an emblem or symbol.

idiom: the language particular to a community or class; usually refers to regular, "everyday" speech.

immigrants: people who move to and settle in a new country.

indigenous: originating in and naturally from a particular region or country.

industrialization: the process by which a country changes from a farming society to one that is based on industry and manufacturing.

SERIES GLOSSARY

integration: the process of opening up a place, community, or organization to all types of people.

kinship: web of social relationships that have a common origin derived from ancestors and family.

literacy rate: the percentage of people who can read and write.

matriarchal: of or relating to female leadership within a particular group or system.

migrant: a person who moves from one place to another, usually for reasons of employment or economic improvement.

militarized: warlike or military in character and thought.

missionary: one who goes on a journey to spread a religion.

monopoly: a situation where one company or state controls the market for an industry or product.

natural resources: naturally occurring materials, such as oil, coal, and gold, that can be used by people.

nomadic: describing a way of life in which people move, usually seasonally, from place to place in search of food, water, and pastureland.

nomadic: relating to people who have no fixed residence and move from place to place.

parliament: a body of government responsible for enacting laws.

patriarchal: of or relating to male leadership within a particular group or system.

patrilineal: relating to the relationship based on the father or the descendants through the male line.

polygamy: the practice of having more than one spouse.

provincial: belonging to a province or region outside of the main cities of a country.

racism: prejudice or animosity against people belonging to other races.

ritualize: to mark or perform with specific behaviors or observances.

sector: part or aspect of something, especially of a country's or region's economy.

secular: relating to worldly concerns; not religious.

societal: relating to the order, structure, or functioning of society or community.

socioeconomic: relating to social and economic factors, such as education and income, often used when discussing how classes, or levels of society, are formed.

statecraft: the ideas about and methods of running a government.

traditional: relating to something that is based on old historical ways of doing things.

urban sprawl: the uncontrolled expansion of urban areas away from the center of the city into remote, outlying areas.

urbanization: the increasing movement of people from rural areas to cities, usually in search of economic improvement, and the conditions resulting this migration.

INDEX

INDEX

INDEX

INDEX

PHOTO CREDITS

ABOUT THE AUTHOR

Michael Centore is a writer and editor. He has helped produce many titles, including memoirs, cookbooks, and educational materials, among others, for a variety of publishers. He has experience in several facets of book production, from photo research to fact checking. His poetry and essays have appeared in *Crux*, *Tight*, *Mockingbird*, and other print- and web-based publications. Prior to his involvement in publishing, he worked as a stone mason, art handler, and housepainter. He was born in Hartford, Connecticut, and lives in Brooklyn, New York.